D1705468

About the Authors

Jo Lyon is one of the co-founders of Talking Talent, an innovative coaching organisation specialising in helping women throughout their careers, as well as supporting men through the transition into fatherhood. Jo has over a decade of coaching experience and is both an Occupational Psychologist and a qualified Neuro Linguistic Programming (NLP) coach. She has worked for a wide range of FTSE 100 companies in a variety of sectors, and has coached extensively at all levels. She enjoys helping individuals to maximise their potential and to achieve personal and organisational goals.

Jo lives in Oxfordshire with her husband and three young daughters.

Harriet Beveridge is a Director for Talking Talent, with over a decade's experience working with senior leaders in a range of industries. She graduated from Oxford University with a BA (Hons) in Philosophy, Politics and Economics, holds a Certificate and Diploma in Coaching and is also an accredited NLP Practitioner. Harriet worked as a management consultant with Ernst Young, specialising in organisational change. She was then a Principal for seven years with rogenSi, a consultancy specialising in leadership, change and growth. She describes herself as "a magpie" for techniques and approaches, and believes that flexibility is the key to coaching. In addition to her wealth of corporate experience, Harriet also coaches in the wider community and spent four years as a Samaritan counsellor.

Harriet lives in Bath with her partner and two young boys.

Top Tips
for Talented
Working
Parents

Jo Lyon
and
Harriet Beveridge

Matador
5 Weir Road
Kibworth Beauchamp
Leicester LE8 0LQ, UK
Tel: 0116 279 2299
Fax: 0116 279 2277
Email: books@troubador.co.uk
Web: www.troubador.co.uk/matador

ISBN 978 184876-809-3

British Library Cataloguing in Publication Data.
A catalogue record for this book is available from the
British Library.

Printed in the UK by

Matador is an imprint of Troubador Publishing Ltd

About Talking Talent

Talking Talent is a niche coaching consultancy which helps companies to:

- retain and progress their talented women through the "pinch points" in their careers
- support employees who are working parents

Why?

In order to:

- Minimise unwanted attrition of key talent
- Save the costs of replacing talent
- Promote gender diversity (research by McKinsey, London Business School and others show benefits such as increased innovation and performance) (Company, 2007) (Business, 2007)
- Quicken the 're-engagement' of maternity returners, to both their role and the business
- Reduce the risk of expensive litigation and divisive disputes

How?

We use three approaches:

- One-to-one and group coaching: giving individuals a safe space to figure out how to navigate change
- Consultancy: diagnosis and design to create cultures and innovative policies & practices that help working parents perform at their best
- Development programmes: rich, highly interactive workshops which enhance behaviours and increase skills

Want to find out more?

Contact us at *www.talking-talent.com* or on 01865 400087

Acknowledgements

The authors would like to acknowledge everyone who helped in putting together this Top Tips book, including all the Talking Talent team – Chris Parke, founder of Talking Talent, for his input to many of the chapters, Nicola Jones for her valuable additions, Astrid van Waveren for bringing it all together, Katie Mossman for co-ordinating key parts – and our partners at OneFishTwoFish for the images we have included, as well as the team at Matador. A special thanks goes to Jane Adshead-Grant and Simon Tarry for their valuable contributions and ongoing support. Finally we would also like to extend our thanks to all the women and men who have participated in our coaching, shown commitment to achieving their personal goals, and who have given such wonderful feedback.

Contents

This book is...

- A treasure trove of hints and tips to help you balance parenthood and work
- Insights from specialist coaches, senior professionals and experienced parents
- An encapsulation of the key topics we've helped over a thousand coachees with over the last five years
- A self-coaching resource to help you reflect on and apply the tips to your context

How this book is structured...

The book is arranged around 15 key topics. For each topic there is:
- An introduction
- A list of tips
- A real life quote from Senior Managers who have navigated the highs and lows of balancing work and parenthood already
- Some coaching questions - these are questions you can ask yourself, to think a bit more deeply on the topic and unlock your own answers

Introduction

There is a lot of unnecessary noise and confusion when moving through a complex transition like being a working parent. At times it can seem like a very emotive topic, and one that everyone has an opinion and advice on – some will resonate, but some will appear insensitive and won't feel right for you. Look at the tips in this book and see which ones are right for you and ignore those which don't feel appropriate for your life.

It's important to have clarity on what is important for you. If you don't have clarity, you may end up feeling inauthentic, guilty, de-motivated or disengaged, and it will not be sustainable.

The purpose of this book is to help you achieve this clarity and think about how to make your personal and professional life work for you.

When working through each section, you will start to think about:

- What are the most important things for you to achieve in order to fulfill your identities as a working parent?

- What do you need to stop doing?

- What do you need to start doing?

- What do you need to do more of?

1

What do you want from work and home?

We all have a sense of who we are and the roles we play, such as professional, partner, sportsperson or community member. How does the role of 'parent' fit into the picture? There may be some conflicts between this new role and our existing sense of ourselves. For example, how can we give adequate time and attention to both our children and our career? How can you bring together being firm and resilient at work when you also want to be a warm, loving parent?

We need to step back and understand what our different roles mean to us and look at where the conflicts might be for us personally. In the past, being a good professional might well have meant working long hours whenever required. Was this really necessary? How do we want to manage this now we are a working parent?

Our definitions of what a good professional or good parent 'should do' will be instrumental in shaping how we manage our working lives.

Why? If we have clarity on who we are and what is important to us, it is much easier to translate this into our day-to-day lives.

Tips
1. Reflect on what's important to you. If you know

what your priorities are it's much easier to translate them into day-to-day actions.

2. Think about where your definitions of "good parent" and "good professional" came from. For example, if we work full time, but had a mother who was available to us 24/7, and are holding that up as a standard for ourselves, we are setting ourselves up to fail.

3. Compare what is on your list for "good parent" and for "good professional". Notice the potential conflicts.

4. Remember a time when you changed role (e.g. from student to professional, or from team member to manager). What helped you make the transition then? Which of these strategies might help you now?

5. Look for role models. Who do you know who manages the multiple roles well? What strategies can you copy from them?

6. Go easy on yourself! Change takes time.

"Returning to work after your first child is traumatic. Having someone independent, knowledgeable and patient to discuss all the emotional, professional and practical issues that arise is indispensable."
Director, International Financial Conglomerate

"Changing my approach to the way I think about things has been really helpful. I now will be pro-

active in order to achieve what I want; I want to take the responsibility for my happiness. Talking through my approach about my next career opportunity and identifying what is really important to me makes me feel more relaxed about having the conversations with my manager. I developed a network of friends, realised I already have some good friends and can be more pro-active in developing these relationships. I no longer feel anxious about being lonely or unfulfilled, I can take responsibility for the way I feel."

Coachee, Magic Circle Law Firm

Coaching questions

- What are your key roles?
- What does "good" look like for each role?
- For that to happen, what needs to be in place?
- What might get in the way? How can you get around these obstacles?

2

Role models

Role models are a great way to start to think about how we can balance our lives better. We can copy the strategies they use, learn from their mistakes and use them for ongoing advice and moral support.

Everyone is different, with individual values and priorities, and different working styles or contexts, so a role model for one person might not be a role model for someone else.

Could you be a role model for someone else? It is still difficult to find a good variety of role models in most businesses. If you were being a role model, what would you be doing? What messages would you be giving and how would you be interacting with others in your business?

Why? Copying other people's strategies can be a quick and easy way for us to achieve better performance and happiness. Being a role model for others can give them the knowledge that being a talented working parent is achievable.

Tips
1. Think about people you know who you feel get the balance right, or elements of the balance right.

2. *Ask* them how they make it work. People are usually very flattered to be asked for advice, even when we don't know them that well.

3. Go beyond the obvious – it's easy to make

assumptions about how people make it work, but getting to the specifics can uncover some surprising answers.

4. Find out about what the role models *do,* but also what they believe and what they think is important. For example, maybe they manage to leave the office on time so they can bath the children because they've put some practical things in place, such as blocking out their diary. Or maybe it's because they strongly believe that the kids will grow up quickly and it's a case of now or never.

5. Be open-minded; if we want to get different results, we need to try different things, but it's very easy to dismiss novel ideas before we've even tried them.

6. Experiment – put the ideas into practice for a trial period and then reflect on what's worked.

7. Offer to be a role model for others.

"Talk to other working parents as they are full of good ideas. Keep positive and be less perfectionist."
Coachee, Investment Bank

"My coach had experienced many of the emotions and issues that I seemed to be faced with and her empathy, delivered in a very positive and reinforcing way, helped me to realise that such feelings are normal and to be expected. In a senior position, the maternity process can feel very isolating and coaching helped me to see that

it is acceptable to want and feel deserving of a career, giving often very practical suggestions of how to manage time so that I can spend as much quality time as possible with my family."

HR Professional, Leading European Financial Services Company

Coaching questions

- Think back; who has really impressed you?
- If you were being a good role model what would you be doing?
- Who have you loved working for as a working parent?
- What did you admire?
- Paint a picture of the ideal role model of a working parent; what does it look like?

3

Longer term career/life planning

We can get so caught up in measuring the countdown to the birth and our babies' progress in terms of months, that our whole focus becomes short term. It can be useful to think longer term about our goals for the next year, five years, or even ten years. Otherwise we run the risk of waking up in a few years' time to find that our career has stalled, or that we are stuck with a work-life balance we hate.

Long term planning doesn't mean you have to know all the answers and it doesn't mean you have to be rigid about things. It can be as simple as recognising what you do and don't know, and deciding the best way forward.

Why? Long term planning helps us focus our energies to achieve the goals we want. It also helps us anticipate and reduce the challenges along the way.

Tips
1. Think about your personal goals over the longer term – e.g. moving house, having more children, or studying for a qualification.

2. Talk with your partner to understand their long term aspirations.

3. Get your thoughts down on paper. Draw a timeline to see how your collective goals match up.

4. Think about how you want your career to progress over the next five to ten years.

5. Build in simple activities now that will help you in the future. For example, if you are looking to change roles, this might be the right time to start networking or researching. It's easier to do these types of activities little and often.

6. Think about your passions, what you are good at and what type of work-life balance you want to achieve. Think creatively about how you can honour each of these drivers.

7. Be clear about what's important to you; what are your drivers or values at work and at home? Use these as a 'compass' to help you choose a path ahead.

"Drawing a timeline on paper made things less scary. I realised that there were some simple things I could do to invest in my future – I think I'd put it into the "too difficult" bucket before."
Coachee, Financial Services Institution

Coaching questions

*   If you keep following the path you are on now, how will things look in five years' time?
*   Are you happy with that?
*   For you to get the future you want, what do you need to stop, start and continue doing now?

4

Securing promotion

Many women assume that it's simply not possible to get promoted whilst pregnant, on maternity leave or soon after the return to work. This is not true, but it can feel challenging to be out of the loop for what seems like a long time. Similarly, men are often worried that they might be taking on too much if they go for promotion when they embark on parenthood.

Before we pursue the promotion route, we need to make sure we want it. For example, what will promotion mean in terms of demands on our time or increases in our stress levels? What compromises might this involve, and are we prepared for them? We need to check what we would be sacrificing to put in the extra effort, and reflect on whether it's worth it for us personally.

If the promotion is right for us, we need to seek it out *actively* – we need to make sure that we've told people that this is what we are working towards. We need to know who our key stakeholders are, who will make the decision and what their expectations of us are. We need to be acting and behaving like the level above us already.

Why? When we are thoughtful and proactive about promotion, we have a much greater chance of achieving our potential and the work-life balance we want.

Tips

1. Reflect on what impact the promotion would have
    on your work-life balance. In some cases promotion
    can, counter-intuitively, make the balance much
    easier because you are allocating workload, rather
    than being on the receiving end of someone else's
    allocation.

2. Make sure that the decision-makers know you want
    promotion. Tell them early on.

3. Be proactive and gather the evidence – create a
    clear business case.

4. Ask others for their advice on how to progress your
    career. Asking for advice is a great way of
    networking – people are usually flattered to be
    asked.

5. Be clear and set a goal for your career.

6. Think creatively about what projects you can get
    involved in which will raise your profile.

7. Know what operating at the next level up looks like.
    Compare it to your current performance and identify
    any potential gaps.

8. Recognise what activities are critical to success in
    your role and culture, and which tasks are self-
    imposed.

9. Review how you work and what you do and don't
    enjoy.

10. Put in place a plan around your goals and how you will achieve them.

"Be strong and confident about what you want and expect in your career."

Coachee, Global Investment Bank

"Coaching really made me think about all of my goals both from a personal and professional perspective."

HR Professional, Leading Global Mobile Telecommunications Company

Coaching questions

- Who needs to know that you want a promotion?
- Whose support do you need to secure a promotion?
- If you were now at the level above, what would you be doing differently from what you are doing now?
- What evidence (e.g. facts, feedback, deliverables, behaviours...) can you give to prove you have reached the required level?

5

Flexible working

Getting enough time at work to do a quality job, and enough time at home to fulfil our standards of being a "good" parent/partner and so on, can be extremely hard. How flexible we can be will depend on our role, our company culture, what our colleagues are prepared to cover and whether we need to be working at particular times.

One option is to consider a formal flexible working arrangement. It can take many different forms and guises. For example:

- Part time working, e.g. working fewer days each week
- Increased holidays, e.g. to coincide with school holidays
- Reduced hours, e.g. working a shorter working day
- Working from home for a number of days per week or month
- Compressed hours, e.g. compressing 5 days into 4 much longer days
- Flexitime; taking time off in lieu of extra time worked.

But for many of us, full time working is the reality, and this is often in the context of a long-hours culture. Work-life balance then becomes less around *reducing* hours and more around how we *schedule* the hours or *manage* our time. So, this might mean leaving at five in order to see our child, but then logging back on when they've gone to bed.

It is important to understand how we feel about flexibility, and what we would and would not be prepared to do. Also, if there is something urgent, how might we be able to respond to that and what notice might we need?

Why? When we get the balance right, the arrangement is sustainable. If it's not right, we risk hugely negative consequences such as under-performance and unhappiness.

Tips

1. Think creatively; what arrangements might work for both you and your employers – even if they haven't been tried before?

2. Consider simple steps that might be easy to achieve and make a big difference – e.g. "I commit to being home one day a week to make bath time".

3. Read up on time management techniques to make the best use of the time you have (e.g. clear prioritisation, planning, delegation...)

4. Install Skype on your computer and say goodnight virtually when you can't be there in person.

5. Make the time spent at work and home focussed and deliberate. Be present and don't allow one to "leak" into the other (see below for more ideas on "managing days you are not working").

6. Discuss your flexible working options with colleagues to understand how it might impact on them.

7. Talk with your partner around how flexible they can be and how you can support each other.

8. Explore the possibility of working from home on occasions to cut out commuting time.

9. Think about childcare options to support the kind of flexibility you might need.

10. Set clear boundaries around work/non-work time.

11. Have a clear idea of what you are happy to flex your boundaries for – e.g. what constitutes an "emergency" that you could stay late for?

12. Get buy-in from key individuals around how you will manage your flexibility.

13. Block time out of your diary so that people don't book meetings at crunch times.

14. Sometimes it's easy to slip into feeling out of control. Remember that you are ultimately in the driving seat about how you live your life. Make an active choice; are you comfortable with your work-life balance? If not, what can you choose to do to improve the situation?

"Make sure you talk to your work as soon as you can about the role you want to come back to,

about their expectations of you and what you want, in terms of flexible working."

Coachee, Financial Services Firm

Coaching questions

- Whose support do you need to make this happen?
- What specifically do you need from them, and what are you giving in return?
- What concerns might key stakeholders have?
- How can you manage their concerns?
- What will stop you achieving flexible working?
- What will enable you to achieve your desired flexible working pattern or style?

6

Managing days you are not working

Parents who try to implement work-life balance boundaries – or those who work part time or flexibly - often feel guilty as they leave the office to colleagues' comments, such as "off already?" or "have a lovely day off tomorrow". For many working parents this undermines the reality of what their non-working time holds. Time with a child is often fun, but certainly not a chance to kick back and relax.

So, how do we manage our time off? How do we manage our own and others' expectations? A lot of this will be guided by what we think is and is not acceptable, as well as what we want and don't want to get involved with in this time.

When looking at how working parents work best, being clear about how they separate their time is key: work time and family time. If work time leaks into family time on a regular basis it can start to create stress and irritation with work and also family. For example, if we leave the office at five to be there to put our child to bed, but then try to answer five emails whilst they are demanding a bedtime story, we're likely to get annoyed with them. Managing the separation between work and home well enables us to manage our emotions more effectively and to do what we do well.

Why? Managing our time off effectively allows us to

spend focussed, quality time on both home and work, which in turn improves our performance and satisfaction.

Tips

1. Turn off your Blackberry, email or phone while you are not working, or allocate specific times of the day to check them if you need to.

2. Be present – have the attitude that you'll focus on your child exclusively. For example, focus on them for the bedtime hour, even if you have to log back on in an hour's time.

3. Who else can do this – can anyone at work filter your emails and only contact you if something is urgent?

4. Have something planned for at least part of your time away from the office, so you are non-contactable and having fun.

5. Make sure time off does not become full of chores – look at the "creating time to focus" section for tips on managing your home 'to do' list.

6. Remember, it will take time to educate yourself and others around how you work now – it could take three months for people to realise you don't work on a Friday, or are going to leave at 5.30 every Tuesday. Be persistent.

7. Push back and ask people if things are urgent and get deadlines.

8. Be flexible when something important comes up - if you can.

9. Be positive when you can't do it, e.g. "that sounds like a great opportunity and although I can't do it today I can help you on Monday" or "If you need urgent help today I suggest you try person X or option Y...".

"Coaching helped me realise the importance of being more specific in terms of needs and expectations (specifically with regard to team members, hand over and transitioning the return), as well as speaking out and forward planning. We talked about asking for the seat on the tube rather than expecting others to offer, and mapping this across into other areas of work."

Coachee, Magic Circle Law Firm

Coaching questions

- Who is driving you to look at your email/answer calls when you are at home? You or someone else?
- What is urgent and needs attention during your time off and what is not?
- What constitutes a legitimate work "emergency" that you will attend to? How can you describe it clearly to your stakeholders?
- Who can cover for you and support you in the office, to allow you to switch off when you are not there?

7

Managing colleagues

It is only through effectively influencing and managing others that we can hope to achieve what we want as a working parent.

For example, we need to make sure our boss and peers are on side with how we are going to work. They need to understand our intentions and constraints. They need to feel valued and that we are taking them into account, not just ourselves. For example, you might be planning on leaving at 5pm every day but do not realise that means one of your colleagues will not be able to go to their favourite tennis drill. It might be fairly simple for you to flex your arrangements one night so your colleagues remain content.

We not only need to manage and maintain our relationships with colleagues internally, but also our external network. It is useful to think through who is in our network and to create a plan of how to keep connected with these individuals. It can be tempting to not focus on this when we have many other priorities already.

Why? To perform well at work and to achieve the balance we want, we need strong working relationships, this will also open up options for us in the future.

Tips
1.   Whether it is in your official job description or not,

include "managing stakeholders" as a key part of your job.

2. Identify the key stakeholders. Go beyond the obvious (boss, team members, peers, clients...) and think about who you need to influence to make things a success in the longer term too (your boss' boss? Your boss' peers?)

3. Put yourself in other people's shoes. See how the world looks from their point of view. What concerns do they have? What assumptions? What standards?

4. Be proactive. *Anticipate* other people's concerns and demands.

5. Make sure key stakeholders know you and see you regularly. Find reasons to pop your head around the door and opportunities to work together.

6. Build a profile by attending external conferences, giving internal talks and publicising your successes.

7. Build your reputation by delivering top quality work and sharing the findings/learnings.

8. Keep building your network – organisational structures change so don't put all your eggs in one basket.

9. Get involved in high profile projects.

10. Maintain your professional network – email people regularly.

11. Catch up with key individuals over coffee or lunch.

"Coaching really made a difference to the way I felt about both going on maternity leave and also returning to work. It wasn't just about me though - I hope the people I work with found the transition to working with my maternity cover and my return to work smooth. It's a challenging time for even the most organised of people and coaching was a great support."
Head of Learning & Development, National Law Firm

Coaching questions

- Who are the key stakeholders who will influence the success of your work pattern?
- What conversations do you need to have with them?
- What messages do they need to hear?
- What questions do you need to ask?
- How can you uncover what they think is working and what their concerns might be?
- Who might be in your external network?
- How do they view you and your relationship?
- What do you need to do to maximise these relationships?

JIM! GOOD TO SEE YOU BUDDY!! HEY, NO BAD NEWS TODAY, I JUST DON'T THINK I COULD HANDLE IT... RIGHT BIG GUY?!
WELL, NOT BAD NEWS JOE, BUT I'D LIKE TO TAKE SOME FAMILY LEAVE.
HOW CAN YOU DO THIS TO ME JIM?! I THOUGHT WE WERE A TEAM! YOU ARE LETTING US DOWN JIM!
SOB SOB!

8

Managing stress

When we have got a lot of different things to think about, our tolerance for one extra thing is low. For many working parents, we are already thinking about our child/children, childcare, the house, bills at home, our work, our work relationships, our objectives, our work commitments... So, there is not a lot of capacity for anything extra. One extra thing can send us into a stressed space. How we deal with this is critical to feeling in control and making sure we resolve it as quickly as possible.

Remember, for most of us, stress at work and at home normally comes in waves and will pass in time. It is most difficult when the waves come together and are longer than expected.

It is really important to try and make sure you have some extra capacity to deal with times of extra stress. It may also be important to make sure you have a good support network in place at work and at home to help you cope.

Why? Managing stress helps us to protect our health and wellbeing, and promotes better efficiency and perform-ance.

Tips
1. Remind yourself that "this will pass" when you are going through a bad patch.

2. Ask yourself "what can I do?", "how can I influence the situation?" and let go of things that are outside your control.

3. Check your body language. Drop your shoulders, unclench your jaw and smile.

4. When you feel overwhelmed, exhale slowly for three breaths – let the in-breaths take care of themselves.

5. Figure out what support you need; do you need to vent to a sympathetic ear? Do you need coaching to help you clarify solutions? Do you need practical help around the home to free up your time, so you can re-charge your batteries?

"Don't worry about feeling stressed and losing confidence about your abilities back at work. It will take a while but it comes back."
Coachee, Investment Bank

"Straightforward and practical advice made my transition back to work after my maternity leave a less daunting experience."
HR Professional, Magic Circle Law Firm

Coaching questions

*   Where do you feel stress physically? What impact does this have?
*   If you were to remove one cause of stress from your life, what would it be?

- What support do you need, so you have the capacity for that one extra thing?
- On a scale of one to ten, where are your stress levels? Some stress is helpful to drive us, but where do you want your stress levels to be?
- What is the biggest contributor to stress?
- Who can you speak to for support?
- How have you handled stress before?
- How easy, on a scale of one to ten, do you find it to say no or to ask for help?

9

Choosing the right childcare for your job

When you have your first child, you realise how important childcare is going to be to your working life going forward.

As working parents, we all experience the months when our child or children seem to be sick all the time. These times are challenging, but it is the way we deal with them that helps define us as professionals and working parents. Having a back up plan for these times is critical to making a challenging job work. Knowing when you need to be with your child is critical to being the parent you want to be.

There are lots of different childcare options out there; choosing the one which is best for you is the key. If you know your child is happy and in safe hands, it means you can focus effectively at work, rather than feel guilty. If you and your partner work long hours, make sure you think through how you are going to make this work. A lot of our decisions on childcare will depend on the back up we have around us. If we have parents who live close, we will be in a different position than if our parents and support network all live abroad.

Reflect on your values, hopes and fears – do you want your child in a group setting, or one to one setting? Some people like the idea of their child being in a social group, others like the one to one attention of a nanny or childminder.

Lastly, remember the cost implications of different childcare will vary vastly. What you do with one child might differ from what you do with more than one.

Why? When we know our children are safe, happy and progressing well with the right childcare, we feel infinitely happier and more relaxed. It's also then much easier to focus and do a great day's work.

Tips
1. Give feedback to your childcare around what you want to know from them, e.g. what your children did in the day, what they ate, etc.

2. Plan a settling-in period and observe your childcare on an ad hoc basis.

3. Be clear what you want your child to be doing, e.g. singing, etc.

4. Make sure your childcare arrangements fit with you and your partner's working hours.

5. Research the options – visit local nurseries and look at the latest Ofstead inspection report online, look online for nanny and nanny share agencies, ask your local council for a list of registered childminders...

6. Plan ahead; waiting lists can be extremely long.

7. Think creatively. Many parents use a mixture of providers – e.g. mother-in-law on Mondays and Fridays, and nursery on the other three days.

8. Think about location – how will you combine drop off and pick up from childcare with your commute to work? Factor in rush hour travel times.

9. Recognise that the childcare you need will change over time depending on the age and number of children you have.

10. Have a backup plan if your childcare is sick, such as a support network. Does your work have an emergency childcare option? What friends or relatives could help?

11. See what support your work offers, e.g. childcare vouchers, working parents' forums, options to buy more holiday...

"Work out in advance of your return to work what your challenges are going to be."
Coachee, Magic Circle Law Firm

"The most valuable piece of advice I received was to start my daughter's childcare a couple of weeks before going back to work, so that both of us had time to adjust, and I wasn't worrying about how she was finding nursery on my first day back at work."
Coachee, Global Law Firm

Coaching question

- If you could choose the best childcare for your child/children, what would it look, feel and be like for you and them, and what environment would they be in?

10

Managing your network outside work

As a working parent, we interact with an intricate web of people outside of work too: our little one/s, our childcare provider, in-laws and other local parents. Many of us do not spend time thinking about who we need to nurture, or how we could best communicate with them, yet this can make all the difference.

Why? When we have a good network we can focus fully on work when we are at work, and we are less likely to get tripped up when there's an emergency.

Tips
1. Find out what expectations your family (e.g. parents and in-laws) have about how often they see your children. You can then be proactive about managing any mismatches in your expectations and theirs.

2. Think creatively about how to involve your family in a way that works for all of you. For example, buy webcams and use Skype to make far away relatives feel connected to the new family, or book in family visits far in advance so you are on the front foot.

3. Reflect on what would have to be in place for you to feel comfortable leaving your child with parents/in-laws/etc. for appropriate periods of time. This will allow them to connect and will give you a break.

4. Be clear with your childcare provider about what's important to you and what you expect from them.

5. Schedule in reviews with your childcare provider to talk about what's working well and what would make the arrangement even better.

6. Ask your children what "quality time" means to them. It's surprising how frank and insightful the answers are from even very young children.

"Plan carefully and always keep discussing things with your husband/partner and family."
Coachee, Financial Services Firm

Coaching questions

- How do you think your network outside of work view you?
- How can you strengthen their understanding of you and your understanding of them?
- What would allow you to ask for help?

11

Creating time for focus

Research shows that managing the home is one of the greatest challenges for working parents. We are doing a demanding job, trying to look after the children and also run the home.

We need to make sure we're not setting ourselves up to fail. We're unlikely to be effective if we are sitting at our desk, but in the back of our mind we're worrying: "What do I need to buy? What am I going to cook? When am I going to do the cleaning? How am I going to see my sister, and when can I work late?..."

If we first identify all the things on our 'to do' list, then we can ask ourselves who else can support us. For example, what's the appropriate split between ourselves and our partner? What can we 'outsource'? What favours can we trade with friends and family?

Why? By simplifying our 'to do' list we can focus on what's really important, and reduce the chances of home worries damaging our ability to perform at work.

Tips
1. Share out the responsibility for cooking and shopping – which do you enjoy?

2. Cleaning – how are you going to get this done? Is it

worth getting a cleaner, if you can afford it?

3. Timebox chores – do a "power hour" of cleaning, or admin, or gardening, for example. When the alarm goes at the end of the hour, *stop*!

4. Diarise activities – e.g. make Monday night ironing night and Wednesday night admin night, so you aren't worrying about it at other times.

5. Give yourself a break – e.g. skip cooking once a week by having a take-away or ready meal.

6. Buy clothes that are easy to iron.

6. Create a list of your quickest, easiest meals and create a menu planner which you can repeat on, say, a fortnightly basis.

7. Consider what the "easy" option might be, without compromising on quality, e.g. 5-minute cous-cous versus 20-minute rice.

8. List all household chores and assign them to someone.

10. Cooking for your child/children – freeze food so you always have a stock in the freezer.

11. Make it easy to clear your home of clutter and make it look nice. Have boxes you can quickly chuck toys into, in-trays for admin and a large dirty clothes basket!

12. Let go of tasks you feel you ought to do but are not vital.

"It was helpful to put some structure and order into my thinking, all my plans have been thrown up into the air and being so busy, I have not had a chance to properly internalise the implications. It has helped me be clearer on what is important to me and to consider other opportunities as to what is possible, which has helped to reduce stress."

Coachee, Global Law Firm

Coaching questions

- What one thing that you do at home could you give to someone else to do tomorrow?
- What activities is it worth letting go of, in order to spend more time on the important things?

12

Making sure you have energy

As a working parent we have little time to think about anything, let alone ourselves. Every now and then we may feel overwhelmed and not know why. We are busy looking after everyone else - work colleagues, partner, children - but who looks after us?

Often we don't make time for ourselves- for weeks or even months at a time. When we work we often feel that any spare time we have should be dedicated to the kids. It can be difficult to do even the simple things for ourselves like having a haircut.

This may work in the short term but in the long term we are in danger of neglecting to fulfil crucial parts of who we are. We end up feeling resentful and exhausted. If we don't look after ourselves, we are no good to anyone else – it's not selfish, it's necessary. What used to give us a buzz does not need to be a thing of the past. What is it for you? Exercise, reading, relaxation, socialising...? Think about how you can recapture some of that *joie de vivre* and personal growth. Remember, it does not have to be a whole day's commitment; spending half an hour on ourselves can make a huge difference to how we feel.

Why? Looking after ourselves is critical if we are going to have the energy we need for work, home and children.

Tips

1. Book time for 'me' in the diary – treat it with the importance you would a business meeting with a client.

2. Get creative – make the most of snippets of time, e.g. listen to music on your commute, or a stimulating podcast, or read a book.

3. Eat properly. Have breakfast and use short cuts to get your five a day. For example, have dried fruit or smoothies.

4. Relax in the bath with a book or magazine and the door shut, or allow yourself to "veg" in front of the TV.

5. Go to the pub with your friends, join a book group or see a movie.

6. Commit to a regular exercise class, join the local five a side football or squash ladder.

7. Go off for part of a day at the weekend and do something for you.

8. Buy a book on meditation or relaxation techniques.

9. Set a goal for yourself, e.g. train for and run a race for charity.

"As a third time mother I was very sceptical that there was anything that I needed help with, as I returned to work to the same employer for the

third time and into a role I knew well. The challenge of three children, however, proved more difficult than I had appreciated - the logistics were fine - long standing nanny who I have great confidence in and an employer who was always flexible and supportive of the hours that I do. The reality, however, was that we were operating on the edge - everything was just about right, but I did not appreciate that it would not take much for things to fall apart around us, and therefore I had not invested much time in thinking about what needed to change. I had put myself at the bottom of the list, and my overwhelming priority was the children, then my husband, then finally me. My physical and emotional energy levels were depleted, and difficulties at work, which with hindsight I should have seen coming, became very difficult to deal with. My usual strength and resilience was gone. My coach worked to help me recognise the situation I was in, and to reappraise what I wanted from the whole work/family/life balance. She was able to convince me to think a bit more selfishly about what I wanted to achieve and what was most important for me.

From my employer's perspective it has also meant that they have retained someone they think highly of, and it helped put their changing requirements and my increasing personal commitments, into a new framework. There is still more to do, but now I know what needs to be done and that the responsibility is mine to make this work."

Director, Global Investment Bank

Coaching questions

- The crew on a plane tell us that if the air supply fails we need to put on our oxygen masks before helping anyone else. How can you make sure you get your "oxygen" in your everyday world?
- What simple steps can you take towards looking after yourself?
- In your wildest dreams what would a treat look and feel like?

13

Managing work with little sleep

For many new parents, whether it is our first, second, third or more child, we will probably experience periods of sleep deprivation. The odd night feels manageable, but ongoing lack of sleep is debilitating and leaves us feeling that we won't be able to deal with the day.

In the long term our babies/children will sleep better and, in fact, we will be trying to force *them* out of bed. In the short term, we need to do all we can to make sure we get enough sleep to function effectively and manage all the things we have on our plate.

It can feel challenging to get the balance right between ourselves and our partner, and it can be a source of controversy or debate – who has had less sleep than whom?

We also need to remember that some people genuinely cope better with little sleep than others. Some of this is physiological, but some is also psychological. Our attitude can help us deal with sleep deprivation more positively. For example, appreciating that it is a temporary challenge can lift our mood. It's also helpful when we can understand *why* it is happening and devise an action plan to improve the situation.

Why? We need enough sleep in order to maintain performance and stay healthy.

Tips

1. Reflect on what's *causing* your child to sleep badly. Is it hunger? Wanting comfort? Because they've started having nightmares? Are they afraid of the dark? Keep a sleep diary to help you spot triggers and patterns of behaviour.

2. Get some respite. Who could look after your child – even for 45 minutes – so you can nap?

3. Take it in turns with your partner to get up in the night or have lie-ins at the weekend.

4. Grab any chance you get. For example, snooze on the train/bus and set the alarm on your mobile phone so you don't miss your stop.

5. Get help, e.g. investigate your local sleep clinic or sleep counsellor (your Doctor or Health Visitor may be able to refer you).

6. Read up on the subject and find an approach that you feel comfortable with. For babies it might be Gina Ford's "Controlled Crying", or Elizabeth Pantley's "No-cry sleep solution", and for older children it might be using reward charts or introducing clocks that show the difference between awake time and sleepy time.

7. Improve the *quality* of your sleep. Relax in the evening before bed, e.g. take a bath or do a minute of slow, relaxed breathing.

8. Go to bed early. Ask yourself what's stopping you from doing this and take action to remove the

obstacles – e.g. if you are cleaning and washing, who else could help you with this?

9. Remember, even though it might feel like a long time, in the long run children will start to sleep better.

10. Remember to share where you are at with others – it is not your work colleagues' fault you are not sleeping well, and they may not understand why you have low energy at work.

"The hardest thing for me when I returned to work after my third child was the lack of sleep I was getting. Some nights I was up 3 or 4 times in the night with different children. It is amazing how you manage to pull yourself together when you get to work and actually what you can achieve when you have had little sleep."
Co-founder of Talking Talent

Coaching questions

- What would it take for you to get a good night's sleep?
- What would make it worth it?
- Who could help you to achieve this?
- How can you be more positive about your sleep?

14

Relationships in a dual career family

Our relationship with our partner is critical to our good health and support in this challenging time. Whether your partner is male or female, you need to make sure that you are paying attention to their needs and your needs as a couple, not just as a parent. This will enable you both to achieve what you need to at home and work.

Research shows that one of the areas which is impacted most by being a working parent, is our relationship with our partner. Before we became parents we still had capacity in the evenings and weekends just for each other. Once we have a child/children and are working, this allocation of time is less clear cut.

Think about what you and your partner enjoyed doing together before you had children, and think about how you might be able to replicate parts of this now. Sometimes going out for a drink or dinner can help us recapture part of who we were before children, and help us to reconnect with our adult selves. This is not always possible, and for some, a night in might be what they have always done as a couple and still prefer to do.

One of the biggest blockers around this can be childcare, especially for some first-time parents: "Who can I get to look after my precious baby?" Think about family or friends who you would trust; is there anyone at your childcare provider who knows your child and can babysit? What about setting up a babysitting circle with other people you know with young children?

Talk about this with your partner and plan what you are going to do. Although we can have good intentions, when we go back to work it can be difficult to find the time and energy to organise it.

It is also important to support each other through the challenges of work and home. If you are both aware of the pressures you are each under you can make sure that you support each other appropriately.

Why? A strong relationship requires care and attention, it doesn't just happen by accident.

Tips
1. Book a night out or a night to turn off the TV and chat with your husband/wife/partner.

2. Talk to your husband/wife/partner about the impact that having a child/children has had on your relationship.

3. Make time regularly – at least once a month - to go out and let your hair down with your friends.

4. Book a weekend away with your partner.

5. Cook together.

6. Talk about how you are feeling and your expectations of each other.

7. Let your partner pursue their hobbies/passions and see their friends. Do the same yourself.

8. You both need to thrive alone and together.

9. Find a babysitter (family, friend, childcare professional or neighbour) and arrange a regular day for them to babysit, e.g. the last Friday of every month.

10. Regularly talk with your partner about what is going on and how you are coping.

11. Ask for help if you need it – don't wait for it to be offered.

"Be prepared to make choices. What is the family model, who else in the wider family will support you with looking after your children – or is it just you and your partner? Different people have different family model ideas. What works best for you?"

Senior Associate, Magic Circle Law Firm

"Ensure you make time for your partner. Talk about medium to long-term requirements, such as booking dentist's appointments, or buying school uniforms, and share the responsibilities. Remember that both your careers are equally important."

Senior Associate, Global Law Firm

Coaching questions

- What are the benefits for you of spending one-on-one time with your partner?
- For you, what would a good night with your husband/wife/partner involve?
- Are you sharing responsibilities?
- Are you discussing your mutual needs?

15

Quality time with your children

When you are working hard and have lots on your mind it can be difficult to think about what to do with your children and how to have fun with them. There may be some days out that you can organise as a family, which you can all look forward to. It also might be useful to put in place regular activities to do with the kids that they can count on – e.g. swimming on a Saturday, or Sunday afternoon at the swings.

Think about how you want to "be" with your children too. For example, we can walk to the playground in a foul mood or an attentive one. Sometimes we get wrapped up in trying to *do* a fun activity, when our kids really just want our attention and engagement, and the activity is of secondary importance to them. Children can also respond well to making a mundane activity fun, or simply being involved. For example, could your children 'help' you do the washing up? Would playing 'I spy' in the supermarket turn it from a chore into something more pleasurable?

Why? Time is precious as a working parent. Thinking about how to have fun with our children can turn even small nuggets of time into quality time.

Tips
1. Talk to your children about their day. What was their favourite thing? What would they like to do again?

2. Read books together.

3. Meet their friends and have them over.

4. Play games with them – there are plenty of books and plenty of internet sites with activities for all ages.

5. Take them for walks.

6. Go to the playground.

7. See the world through their eyes – what would make a 'dull' activity pleasurable for them?

8. Arrange a special family day out, e.g. a picnic by the river, a trip on the train, a trip to a National Trust site, or Lego Land, etc.

9. Attend a regular activity, such as swimming or ballet.

10. Be part of their learning – help with homework.

"Enjoy it! This is a very small period in your life heading to a much bigger and more challenging one."
Coachee, Global Financial Services Firm

"Be creative – my four year old doesn't like getting dressed for preschool, but he loves pretending he's putting a fireman's uniform on. It's utterly daft, but it gets us out of the house and me to work on time and smiling."
Coachee, Investment Bank

Coaching questions

- How do you want your children to remember you in their childhood?
- What would you be doing in order for them to have those memories?

Recognising and overcoming the challenges of being a working parent

There are many stereotypes around being a working parent and these influence our personal experiences of working and having a family. We need to remember that everyone is unique, has grown up in different environments and is influenced by a variety of experiences, values and opinions. So we need to be clear about what is important to us, not what we believe others think is important.

In and out of work we are exposed to a number of different messages consciously or unconsciously from colleagues we work with, clients, peers, managers, partners, parents in law... Everyone has their own view of what is right and wrong, and what a good working parent does and does not do. It is not surprising then that, as working parents, we can feel surprised or confused around what we and others expect of us.

The messages we hear from those around us day to day often become motivators or de-motivators for us.

Time and time again we hear people talking about how they have to work harder to prove themselves once they are a parent. A recent report[1] has also indicated that relationships with peers are impacted once you have children. So, even more reason to be seen to be working longer and harder than non-working parents. The pressure of having multiple important roles can sometimes be daunting and make us feel that we are not performing as well as we really are.

1 Recent research released by *Grazia Magazine*: The Women and Work Survey 2010'

There are also your own individual values that you will constantly refer back to which will inform the way that you work and the way you want to be viewed by your colleagues. Are you a very driven individual? Do you have a strong drive to complete activities you start? Do you have perfectionist tendencies? Is the team very important to you? Are you highly competitive? Do you have a strong sense of integrity? Do you believe that you are the best childcare for your children and everything else will be a failing for them?

Our thoughts about how others see us, and our expectations of ourselves, will shape our experience as a working parent. In the best cases they help to provide clarity, a sense of purpose and of authenticity in the way that you decide to manage your career as a working parent. In the less positive cases they can provide a set of limiting beliefs or negative fantasies about how hard it will be to cope as a working parent in your work relationships and your role. Here are some typical 'inner demons' which are common.

Have you ever found yourself thinking any of the below?
- I will prove having children hasn't made a difference to my effectiveness at work

- I mustn't let my colleagues down by not finishing X and Y

- People will treat me differently now I'm a parent

- I will fail as a parent if I don't stay at home to look after my children

- I'm a poor colleague unless I put the hours in like everybody else

- They love the nanny more than me

- The childcare is taking over my role as a parent/mum/dad

- I can never be the mother/father that my parents/partner want me to be

- I'm not doing anything well – I'm failing as a professional and I'm failing as a parent

- Part-time working is career suicide

- My brain has turned to mush – I won't be able to perform to this level any more

- My friends/family all think I'm a terrible mother because I work full time

- I'm selfish if I do something for me

- My career is less important than my partner's, I must take a back seat

- They will discover that I am a fake

- I'll lose all of my clients

- My role cannot be done flexibly or they will never allow me to work flexibly

- The business just won't cope without me there

- I'll no longer be promoted now I am a working mum/dad.

For many people these thoughts impact on them every day. They affect everything we do, from performing at work, organising a good work-life balance, spending quality time with the children and maintaining good relationships with our work colleagues as well as our support networks.

For some people these can become overwhelming and negative, for others they can become a motivator to do more and better. In both cases they are 'demons' which colour our thoughts and feelings.

So, how can we do things differently? What is the benefit of these thoughts for you? What would happen if you did not think these things again?

It is really important that we reflect on this and really understand what is driving us. If we think we should work 12 hours a day in the office every day, then how will this impact on our work-life balance? If we think we are a failure, how will this impact on our sense of self-worth and effectiveness?

How would we feel if our best friend said some of these things to us? Upset? If we wouldn't like someone else saying these things to us, we should think twice about saying them to ourselves.

Think about the beliefs you have developed around being a 'good professional' and 'good mother'. Check in with them, are they real? Who really thinks them? You, or someone else? If it is you, is it right? Who can give you feedback to check this out? If it is something you think someone else is thinking, ask them – it may be that they are in fact thinking something very different and that the misconception is born from your internal dialogue.

Replace these with more positive messages like:

- I am doing a fantastic job managing my work and life

- I can get what I want out of my work and life

- I am clear on what I want to achieve at work

- I am providing my clients with the service they expect

- I am managing boundaries effectively and people know how to get hold of me.

Conclusion

It is important to know what you want in all aspects of your life. You can do this by being clear around what you really want and by checking that it is realistic. The tips included in this book should help you think about how you can make it happen and who you need to get on board, as well as consider how to organise your work and life to make it possible. Remember to continually review your goals and keep communicating with key people in your life.

The most important thing is to be authentic and true to yourself and your values. If you do what is right for you, then other people will support you and you will have the energy to make it work.

Bibliography

Business, L. B.-L. (2007). *Innovative Potential: Men & Women in Teams.* London: London Business School.
Company, M. &. (2007). *Women Matter.*

Notes

Notes

Notes

Notes

Notes

Notes

Notes

Notes

Notes

Notes

Notes